The Soul of Feminism

Reflections

Marilyn Cornelius

Also by Marilyn Cornelius

Poetry

◊ *One Friend: A collection of Poems*, 2016
◊ *Visionaries: My Life-Changing Mentors*, 2016
◊ *Beyond Blood: Soul Connections*, 2016
◊ *Earth Champions: Birthing a New World*, 2016
◊ *Seasons of Life: Nature's Nurturing Energy*, 2016
◊ *Awakened Living: Transforming Trauma and Embracing Compassionate Change*, 2017
◊ *Meditation: Inspired Moments*, 2017
◊ *Dance: Poems of Passion, Inspiration and Oneness*, 2017
◊ *God is Simple: Reflections and Poems Inspired by Heartfulness Practices*, 2020
◊ *Awakening: The Sacred Order of Divine Poets*, (with incarcerated individuals), 2020
◊ *Eternity Risen*, (with incarcerated individuals), 2021
◊ *High Priestess: Divine Feminine Rising*, 2021
◊ *Heaven is a New Earth: The Nature of Harmony*, 2021
◊ *Namkeen: Ocean of Bliss and Tears*, 2021
◊ *Saying No – Prevailing over Patriarchy*, 2022
◊ *Life's Changing Waves: Love, Empowerment, and Loss*, 2022

Self-Help

◊ *Being S.A.F.E: A Quick Guide to Empowered Communication and Boundary Setting in the Workplace*, 2023

Living and Leading Authentically Framework:
◊ *The Path to Romantic Success: What You Won't Learn in School or at Home about Finding True Love*, 2018

    ◊   *From Abuse to Empowered: Recognizing and Releasing Behavior Patterns that come from Trauma,* 2018

    ◊   *Dimensions of True Self: A Workbook for Living and Leading Authentically* (with Margaret, Nicholas, and Nathaniel Cornelius), 2021

    ◊   *Career Manifestation : What it Takes to be Who You Truly Are in a World that Wants You to be Someone Else,* (with Margaret Cornelius), 2021*

Reflection Guides

    ◊   *Personal and Planetary Wellness: Addressing Climate Change, Health and Social Justice Challenges,* 2017

    ◊   *Angels Who UpLyft: A Celebration of Diversity,* 2018

    ◊   *Sculpting Positivity: Daily Inspirations from the show "Mornings with Marilyn",* 2019

    ◊   *The Four Ethics: Navigating Life Authentically,* 2020

    ◊   *Sculpting Positivity II: A Thought a Day from the show "Mornings with Marilyn,* 2022

*This book is also an autobiography.

Recipe Books

    ◊   *Food of Love: 39 Recipes from my Heart to Yours,* 2015**

    ◊   *World of Love: Delicious Plant-Based and Gluten-Free Cooking Made Simple,* (with Margaret Cornelius), 2017

    ◊   *Flavor of Love: Recipes that Plant Harmony, Grow Wellness, and Feed the Soul,* (with Margaret and Nathaniel Cornelius), 2018

** All books are available via Amazon and/or Kindle, except *Food of Love,* which is available on Book Patch.

   ◊   *Practice of Love: Recipes for Wellness,* (with Margaret Cornelius), 2020
   ◊   *Promise of Love: Recipes that Celebrate Self-Love in all Seasons,* (with Margaret Cornelius),2021
   ◊   *Purpose of Love: Fun Recipes Playing with Flavor and Form,* (with Margaret Cornelius),2021
   ◊   *Treasures of Love: An Abundance of Nutrition, Flavor, and Joy,* 2022
   ◊   *Triumph of Love: The Crowning Glory of Fusing Flavor and Nutrition*
   ◊   *Treats of Love: Vegan, Gluten-Free, No Refined Sugar*

Autobiography

   ◊   *A Fair Way: Finding Balance in an Ever-Changing World,* (with Nathaniel, Nicholas and Margaret Cornelius), 2022

Journals

   ◊   Empowerment Journal, 2022
   ◊   Reflection Journal, 2022
   ◊   Gratitude Journal, 2022
   ◊   Self-Love Journal, (with Margaret Cornelius, Michelle Reddy, and Sidhant Maharaj), 2022
   ◊   Trauma Healing Journal, (with Artika Singh, Kaushal Sharma, and Nicolette Goulding), 2023

Marilyn Cornelius

DEDICATION

For Nic

For all feminists who are working to uproot toxic patriarchal patterns...

Table of Contents

ACKNOWLEDGMENTS

I am grateful to Zumba, which, even when I'm low on sleep, provides energy and inspiration. It was after a Zumba class one dreary Tuesday morning as I sat snacking after a shower, that the idea to compile this book descended on the leaf of my idle mind like a delicate butterfly.

Thank you Michelle, for my return to feminism.

As always, I am grateful to Margaret (Ma) for her willingness and enthusiasm when editing my work. You are simply amazing! Thanks Nic for brainstorming cover ideas with me, and Nathaniel (Dad) and Ma for providing feedback on cover design — I use a hibiscus on the cover that I photographed while in Vanuatu on a climate resilience mission.

Introduction

Feminists are sometimes judged as being too angry, or being man-haters. I can understand anger as a driver for feminist advocates. A few years ago I participated in a feminist march against rape and carried a sign with a friend that said something like, "women are flowers, be gentle". We got some strange looks from people, but after the march many women and girls came up to us to chat about our sign.

Our concept was that we have more tools than anger[1] – we have the universal appeal of love and compassion too. We have the power of owning our vulnerability. Love is a more

---

[1] Anger is an interesting messenger about inner trauma – check out my chapter about anger in this amazing anthology: Patel, K., Ricard, M., Doty, J., Khan, PZI., Vaughn-Lee, L., Elworthy, S., Kumar, S., Carmen, R., Gaspar, V., Cornelius, M., Kannan, V., and Denley. E. "Anger as Trauma's Messenger," *From Anger to Love: A Collaboration from the Fields of Science, Psychology, and the Contemplative Traditions.* Heartfulness Education Trust, 2023.

sustainable vehicle for motivating change than anger. Of course anger is useful too, if channeled into appropriate action. In the long-run, loving compassion and strong boundaries will get us farther than just anger.

For far too long, prominent self-proclaimed feminists, at least in my homeland of Fiji, have used anger as a weapon in their work, and as a shield to cover up the inner issues they won't resolve. They have used their rage to abuse their colleagues and to harm the movement by earning a reputation as toxic. As you can imagine, their approach hurts the feminist movement internally and externally.

I began working as a consultant with feminists many years ago, even before I recognized what feminism meant. As a trauma survivor who began doing serious inner healing in 2015, I realized by 2017 that I had so much patriarchy stuffed into me that I needed a detox. I began to unlearn passivity, people-pleasing, boundarylessness, and many more coping mechanisms I had gathered along the rocky path of my life.

I discovered (trigger warning) that I had been abused as a child, and that this experience had led to my particular coping mechanisms. I decided to discontinue this way of living, uproot my trauma patterns, and begin to live more authentically.

My unlearning, learning, and healing led me to many awakening experiences, and changes in behavior. Now, in 2023, I am a feminist who believes in equal opportunity, a world free of stereotypes and oppression, acceptance of all genders and sexual orientations, and justice above all. I work through coaching, consulting, facilitation, writing and speaking to shed light on how we all have internalized the toxic patriarchy, and how to remove it and move forward in a more empowered way.

Uprooting trauma is a complex endeavor; it's like taking the engine out of a moving car to upgrade and fine tune it while removing large chunks of dirt, cleaning, and adding some sleek, aerodynamic components. These new parts will feel uncomfortable for a while, and later contribute to a feeling of unstoppable-ness.

Yes, I take liberty with my words. And, I would be remiss if I didn't define the terms I am going to be using in this book, *The Soul of Feminism*, in these reflective and reflexive (self-reflective) essays, which includes adaptations of blogs I've written, plus new content. Before I share my own definitions, I wanted to reflect on two excerpts from feminists that have greatly shaped my thinking.[2] I love the following paragraphs from the International Women's Development Agency (IWDA):[3]

"Quite simply, feminism is about all genders having equal rights and opportunities.

Intersectional feminism can seem complicated, but it's really just about acknowledging the interplay between gender and other forms of discrimination, like race, age, class, socioeconomic status, physical or mental ability, gender or sexual identity, religion, or ethnicity.

The barriers faced by a middle class woman

---

[2] Also see the Preface of my book, *Saying NO: Prevailing over Patriarchy* for a summary of my thoughts on patriarchy: https://amzn.to/37eCbAW

[3] Source: https://iwda.org.au/learn/what-is-feminism/

living in Melbourne are not the same as those of a queer woman living in rural Fiji. Women aren't just exposed to sexism – racism, ableism, ageism, homophobia, transphobia, and religious persecution are intrinsically linked to how they experience inequality."

In addition, my all-time favorite definition is this one, which I came across while working with Women's Fund Fiji (WFF):[4]

"Feminism as an ideology believes in the 'Transformation of all social relations of power that oppress, exploit or marginalise any set of people on the basis of their gender, age, sexual orientation, ability, race, religion, nationality, location, caste class or ethnicity'." [5]

When I read this, I had an epiphany and was able to release my biases against the feminism. I had seen too much of the man-hating, angry

---

[4] Learn more about the WFF: https://womensfundfiji.org/
[5] Source: Milliken, E. (2017). *Feminist theory and social work practice. Social Work Treatment: Interlocking Theoretical Approaches;* Turner, FJ, Ed.; Oxford University Press: Oxford, UK, 191-208.

variety of feminism to want to include myself in this community, but this definition opened me to realizing that feminism is about everyone. *Feminism is for everyone. We all benefit from achieving a feminist world, because it means we will all be accepted for who we really are.* What could be more powerful?

Here's a list of terms with what I mean by them – these definitions are my own, intended to simplify and bring clarity to my mind, based on my experiences and reflections:

Feminism: *a way of life that champions and practices equality, works to remove oppression, and builds justice and peace for all people. It is a way of living and working that shares power with others, instead of holding power over others.*

Feminist: *a person who embodies feminism in their personal, professional, social, economic, ecological and other arenas and functions of life.*

Gender: *identity that was typically based on male or female sex but is really about social* and cultural characteristics, along a non-binary a spectrum of identity. This means gender can be fluid and changing; it need not meet any previous norms or stereotypes.

Internalized Patriarchy: the state of having patriarchal thoughts, feelings and behaviors as a powerful internal default that subconsciously controls our interactions, and drives our approach to everything in life and work. For example, the urge to appear strong and never show emotion is internalized patriarchy.

Intersectionality: the interdependent and overlapping nature of gender, race, ethnicity, class, and other issues, requiring us to look at oppression and injustice holistically.

Toxic "Feminists": women who work in the feminist movement and call themselves feminists but abuse power, and abuse their colleagues using patriarchal tactics such as control, manipulation, shaming, gaslighting, and aggression.

Toxic Patriarchy: *a pervasive cultural system that depicts men as superior to women; labels emotions and emotional people, especially women, as weak, requiring men to bottle up emotions. This system creates an unequal society where women and gender non-conforming people are marginalized and treated unfairly.*

Equity: *To have access to the resources and opportunities that a person needs based on their situation and circumstance to reach a just outcome.*

Equality: *To have the same access to the same resources and opportunities as everyone else.*

The essays in this book have two intentions only: to share my views based on my experiences, and to hopefully empower you, dear reader, in your journey.

In Part I, I focus on internalized patriarchy, while Part II is focused on toxic "feminists" who carry deep emotional wounds and inflict pain onto others. Part III contains three case studies based on the first two seasons of the Netflix series Bridgerton, which struck me as a powerful departure from the toxic patriarchy even though it is set in the Regency era of Jane Austen – more on this later. Through the Bridgerton case studies, I draw parallels from the characters and trauma patterns to Pacific examples of feminists using what I call Pacific Spotlights.

In closing, I discuss gaps in gender work in the Pacific, where I am currently based, and provide a set of qualities that I consider to be the soul of feminism.

Each essay, case study, and Pacific Spotlight contains a reflection question or two to guide your journaling.

I wish you an enlightening experience; I hope you leave with more questions and a greater desire to understand and improve yourself than when you started this book.

Yours in solidarity,
Marilyn

November 2023
Suva, Fiji

Marilyn Cornelius

Part I   Internalized Patriarchy

"The first act of violence that patriarchy demands of males is not violence toward women. Instead patriarchy demands of all males that they engage in acts of psychic self-mutilation, that they kill off the emotional parts of themselves. If an individual is not successful in emotionally crippling himself, he can count on patriarchal men to enact rituals of power that will assault his self-esteem."

Bell Hooks

"Patriarchy is so ingrained in our psyche, that most of us propagate it in small ways even without realizing."

Shoojit Sircar

3 Steps to Say NO to Patriarchy

A few years into working with feminists, I had a wakeup call. I realized that toxic patriarchy is alive and well, and I'm swimming in it. That feeling is akin to swimming in insidiously polluted waters, and being told not only is the water pristine, but this is the only water available. I wrote a book as a result of my outright refusal to swim in this toxicity and to chart a course that is centered on love – it is a volume of poetry called *Saying NO: Prevailing Over Patriarchy*.[6]

Patriarchy is a system in which the dominating figure is the (usually white, heterosexual) male, and all others, including females, LGBTQIA+ communities, children, and elders are expected to defer to that male. This system interacts with other factors like religion, race, ethnicity, gender, and socioeconomics to create complex waves of injustice that need to be addressed with attention to this intersectionality.

---

[6] You can find this book here: https://amzn.to/37eCbAW

As a woman of Indian descent born in Fiji who spent half her life in the United States, I've seen more than my share of patriarchal damage. I was also born into a family that had plenty of patriarchal abuse.

A common assumption is that patriarchy benefits men, because they are seen as superior. However, the sad truth is that not only do men oppress everyone else, they also suffer from being conditioned not to show emotion, stay stoic, and be the steady provider. Men suffer heart attacks, strokes, and cancer after bottling up their negative emotions for years. Worse, men who are abused as children can turn into rapists, narcissists, and pedophiles. Where is the benefit of this false sense of superiority?

Regardless of gender, sexual orientation, ethnicity, race, or religion, we must take three steps to overcome patriarchy and forge a new, healthier and more balanced way of life, as the poems in *Saying NO: Prevailing over Patriarchy* portray:

1. **Choose love over fear:** Fear comes from ego, and results in insecurity, anger, aggression, and violence. Love is nurturing, kind, and life-affirming. Choosing love at every step in life ensures that we can stop the cycle of abuse and heal. This is difficult because if we have known only abuse from a young age, love is unfamiliar, uncomfortable, and therefore *unsafe*. We need guidance from a trusted person to go into this new territory of love and turn it into our new norm.

2. **Express our truth:** It is crucial to speak about our honest perspectives, and share our pain, joy, and wisdom. There is no greater release than the expression of authenticity. People often ask me why we need to tell stories of what was done to us. It is so that we can own our truths and be free of them. Whatever we hide, will not let us go.

3. **Embrace the feminine way:** Regardless of your gender, the uplifting of your feminine energy is what will bring

balance to a world choking with toxic masculinity and patriarchy. Some ways to heighten your inner feminine energy and bring it into balance with your masculine energy are: connect with your creativity, create flow states, practice compassion, and set strong boundaries.[7]

Here is one poem from this book to spur you on your journey:

trauma site (excavate)

dear friend
when i speak about the beauty
of the true self
you may feel it's airy-fairy
you may feel it's fake
you see, you simply don't see it
because there are initial steps to take

you started off pure and whole
innocent and beautiful
then you were filled

---

[7] To learn more about boundaries, see my book, *Being S.A.F.E: A Quick Guide to Empowered Communication and Boundary Setting in the Workplace:* https://amzn.to/47DAcR4

with beatings, abusive words and fright
you see, dear friend
you became a trauma site

the first step
and maybe the hardest
is to love all that you are including
the festering effluent of chemical waste
the pollution and shame
the second step is to excavate
all the trauma
relive it and let it leave
the third step is to emerge and discover
your true self
dormant all this time
yes it takes a while
the last step is to unleash
your creativity
authentically
and be all
you were meant to be
it isn't easy
when all of this wants to happen
all at once
slow down, dear friend
think of here, now, today
not the end

that's my story
it's the story of all who

seek heaven
here on earth

so if true self
and self-love
and boundless joy
feel fake
remember, dear friend
it's because you must
love, not hate
all the darkness
that brought you here
to deliberate
and you must
love the process
and take
the time
to excavate

I urge you to discover your own pathway to freedom from this paradigm of oppression. It's time to create a better way, and that can only begin from within.

Reflection:

What might be some first steps you could take to begin to remove patriarchy from yourself?

Notes:

7 Ways to Stop Internalizing Patriarchy

I've noticed in many workshops I've facilitated, that feminists, like the rest of us, have internalized patriarchal ways of being. And, most of us are often unaware of the fact that we are embodying the toxic patriarchy in our daily lives.

So many aspects of life and work are infused with toxic patriarchal norms, expectations, and stereotypes. The need to keep working, to avoid self-care because it's labeled selfish, to not show emotions because we'll be considered weak, or to behave aggressively, neglect family or compete ruthlessly to get promoted. Perhaps the most telling of all is the internalized anger and aggression feminists feel while they work to advance the rights of women, girls and non-binary people.

Put simply, patriarchy is a toxic pool that we all swim in – and sometimes it's so pervasive we don't even realize what is happening. Well, the good news is there are ways to unhook ourselves from the unhealthy ways of patriarchy. Here are seven of them:

1. **Above all, be authentic.** Consider this: if you're not authentic, you won't get anywhere with any quality. Pretense and lies are unsustainable ways of living and working, not to mention exhausting and damaging. Being authentic means discerning, acknowledging and being accountable for the ways in which you are still being influenced by the patriarchy. I administer self-assessments to help workshop participants understand how the patriarchy is affecting them.

2. **Prioritize self-care.** The patriarchy tells us to keep going, keep giving, and keep competing, which is a recipe for burnout. The alternative, and part of the feminist revolution, is to practice self-care diligently, and see wellness as the foundation for living and working in balance. Slow down often, and take care of you.

3. **Heal your past inner wounds.** We all carry the burden of past pain, from events that have left us scarred. Whether

it's sexual harassment, emotional, verbal, physical or sexual abuse, unfair pay, or other injustice at the hands of a toxic and patriarchal boss, we know what we've been through. It's important to heal and release the past, so we can make room for the present, and build the future.

4. **Challenge the status quo.** It's not enough to be aware of the toxic patriarchy, and to take care of ourselves. We must also question and challenge norms that create or perpetuate harm, so we can change the system in which patriarchy still thrives. This means speaking up whenever something is unfair, sexist, and questionable. It means knowing your rights, setting strong boundaries, and enforcing them.

5. **Communicate and act without anger, but with mindfulness.** Anger and aggression are hallmarks of the toxic patriarchy. When we embody harmful masculine energies, we harm the feminist movement instead of nurturing it. It is important to cultivate behaviors and

speech that are encouraging, empathic, and gentle. We cannot help others build solutions while the patriarchy controls us from the inside.

6. **Build a supportive community of friends.** It's crucial to have self-validation, but also to have caring friends around you as sounding boards. A small group of like-minded people can make all the difference in navigating how to remove patriarchy from your own mind.

7. **Choose a guide.** Coaching, therapy, or counseling can be a bridge from your old way of thinking to your new one, giving you the opportunity to rely on a trained individual to help guide you through the messiness of many years of habitual thinking patterns, fears, and biases.

Reflection:

Which of these steps resonate the most with you? Why?

Notes:

The Feminist Paradox: Internalized Patriarchy versus Self-Care

Recently, while heading to a gathering of dynamic women who are advancing the feminist agenda and working hard to make gender equality a reality, I began reflecting on the importance of self-care. The more I work with feminists, the more I notice their dedication, passion, and tireless work to make our world a better place. While it's commendable, there is also a strong foundation of patriarchy buried underneath all that devotion to ending all forms of discrimination against women, girls and gender non-conforming people.

That foundation may contain, on one hand the desire to work nonstop, and not show any signs of "weakness" which is associated with rest and self-care. On the other hand, the endless grooming women put themselves through to appear beautiful by patriarchal standards. In some sense, self-care becomes about men and patriarchy.[8] My observation of

---

[8] For more on this idea, see:
https://www.vogue.in/content/why-is-self-care-for-women-so-much-about-men

the feminists I work with is the former: they work themselves to the bone, carrying guilt that they might not be doing enough. This is, needless to say, a way of working that can never be sustained; we will burn out, over and over.

As a coach, and even as a facilitator, my goal is always to help every person I interact with get closer to their authentic self. This can be very complicated for feminists, because we identify with those who are being persecuted, take on their suffering, and become angry or depressed or cynical. Anger combines with the tendency to push ourselves harder and work in ways that fits nicely with the toxic patriarchy: being stoic; not taking breaks; viewing emotions, slowing down and self-care as signs of weakness; and negatively judging those who show vulnerability. Depression and cynicism can be dangerous, taking us down a slippery slope of apathy – this is when we need to seek help.

We also need to listen to our bodies, and slow down when we are tired and need rejuvenation. This, too, can become complicated by our own trauma – we receive signals from our bodies that spur us on, consciously or subconsciously. For instance, we don't feel safe, or we want to avoid the pain we hold inside. As a result, we overwork, keeping ourselves so busy that we don't have time to acknowledge our real inner state. We don't make time for the inner work we need to do so we can live more authentically. Instead, we stay stuck in patterns that allow traumatic behaviors to linger.

We may also turn to the abuse of food, alcohol, drugs, money, or other addictions as coping mechanisms that hurt us more, causing ongoing accumulation of negative impact. Sadly, many feminists in Fiji, where I am currently based, are abusive to their colleagues, using patriarchal tactics to control, manipulate and destroy the feminist movement from within. This implosion can only be addressed by admitting we need help, and then getting that help.

There is hope, however, and this comes in the shape of new feminist initiatives that uplift self-care and justice for women and marginalized communities — like the work the

Pacific Feminist Fund (PFF) is doing.[9] The trick is to maintain balance as we do this work, lest we submit to achieving ends that the means cannot justify. What good is our effort to uproot patriarchy from society when we have yet to uproot it from ourselves? Surely the inner and outer realities must be healed in tandem.

Reflection:

What steps have you taken to practice self-care?

What remains difficult for you and why?

Notes:

---

[9] Learn more about the PFF:
https://www.linkedin.com/in/pacific-feminist-fund-67b10926a/

Part II Toxic "Feminists"

"Feminism isn't about flipping the script of gender roles, where women are powerful and in charge and men are submissive. Feminism is about increasing the freedom we all have to find the roles that fit us best."

Ginny Brown

3 Reasons Toxic Leaders Can't be Feminists

I have a record number of coaching clients at the moment, and based on their collective experiences and my own, I've been reflecting on what it means to be a feminist.

My reflections on my lived experiences with toxic leaders, and the experiences of my clients have led me to three reasons that toxic leaders cannot be feminist, even if they claim to be:

1. **They abuse power:** Toxic leaders, of any gender, tend to be controlling, manipulative, undermining, as well as emotionally and verbally abusive. They take advantage of empathic and intelligent workers, often taking credit for their work, thereby diminishing career opportunities for these hard workers. This tendency to use their authority unethically and wield power over instead of power with, is the very antithesis of feminism. Anyone who abuses power cannot, by definition, be a feminist.

2. **They are operating from trauma, not authenticity**: Toxic, abusive leaders tend to unleash the negativity they hold inside from their past abuse and lingering trauma – they often do this consciously to hide their insecurity and fear. Their patterns of behavior may include creating trauma bonds, invoking guilt, interspersing abuse with kindness to confuse their victims, extreme rage followed by calm behavior, and other narcissistic or bipolar tendencies. One example is, after berating their workers in front of colleagues, the toxic leader talks to the workers at a later time like nothing has happened; they never apologize for the outbursts. This mode of operation is far from a conscious feminist stance; rather it is a reactionary result of abuse that is being used to torture others.

3. **They clearly exhibit internalized patriarchy:** Many toxic leaders of any gender tend to display classic toxic patriarchal traits: dominance, aggression, controlling behavior, stoicism, and more. They tend to be bullies who overwork

their employees and shame them when they need self-care. This behavior is, again, the opposite of a feminist approach that champions shared power and collective care.

Women leaders who are toxic also cannot be true feminists, because they are using patriarchal techniques to try and further the feminist cause. This is akin to wanting to build a new structure using the old festering foundation – it can never be viable.

True feminist leadership, for me, is the ability to lead with empathy, vulnerability, honesty, integrity, and strong boundaries that uplift all, regardless of gender.

Reflection:

When we support and empower toxic "feminists", we are enabling abuse. Reflect on this statement.

Have you experienced toxic feminism in your life? What might help you/helped you steer clear of it?

Notes:

8 Reasons Feminists might be Assholes

I wanted to reflect more on why feminists can be so difficult to deal with sometimes, even when one is aiming to support them. I work a lot with feminists, and inevitably, as with all my work, it ends up being trauma work, underneath whatever else I am doing.

Of course, there are some incredibly badass feminists out there who actually embody what they want the world to look like, but for the most part, I have encountered many feminists who are harmful to people around them and to their causes. This essay aims to understand why this is the case.

Sometimes, it's hard for people to see how they come across. They fail to see that they are being assholes - I am using Stanford Professor Bob Sutton's definition:[10]

"those who deliberately make co-workers feel bad about themselves and who focus their aggression on the less powerful, poison the

---

[10] Source: https://tinyurl.com/ukw6vyff

work environment, decrease productivity, induce qualified employees to quit and therefore are detrimental to businesses, regardless of their individual effectiveness."

While this definition is quite corporate, it applies to feminists who are so toxic they can lead to other feminists wanting to leave the women's movement – many such women have been or currently are my coaching clients. These women became so traumatized that they approached me for help to clear the low self-esteem, diminished confidence and symptoms of post-traumatic stress from emotional and psychological abuse by their "feminist" supervisors.

Toxic "feminists" may have the best intentions, but their behavior is to some extent controlled by early subjugation, manipulation, abuse, and other toxic patriarchal experiences. Hence, many feminists are often trapped in the very patriarchal, capitalistic and colonialist paradigms they seek to abolish, because their unhealed trauma has become an invisible compass that guides their professional and personal behavior, as we saw in Part I.

While it is important to have compassion for toxic "feminists", it is equally important to set boundaries that prevent you from being harmed. This can be very tricky in the workplace where there are power dynamics. According to McKinsey & Company research, toxic workplace behavior is the leading cause of negative outcomes at work, including burnout and intent to leave one's job.[11]

Here are eight reasons that help explain why feminists, despite all their efforts in working to change the world from a toxic patriarchal one to a peaceful and just one, can be assholes:

1. **Toxic comparison:** As children, parents compare us to our siblings, cousins and other children, quickly cementing in us a sense of ongoing insecurity and "not good enough-ness. This insecurity can lead to constant and toxic comparison to everyone we meet as adults. For feminists, this can manifest as constant

---

[11] For more on this McKinsey research, see: https://www.mckinsey.com/mhi/our-insights/addressing-employee-burnout-are-you-solving-the-right-problem

manipulation, one-upping, and other tactics to try to prove they are better than whichever feminist they are threatened by. Besides being counterproductive to the collaborative, co-leadership and co-responsibility championed and embodied by true feminists, it is a huge waste of energy to be constantly comparing oneself to everyone one meets.

2. **Constant acquisition:** While feminists should seek to empower subjugated voices, they can also consciously or subconsciously seek to acquire the tools, skills, and talents of those they encounter. This can become a colonialist approach: privileged feminists seeking to take what is seen as valuable from marginalized and underrepresented feminists and their communities, and apply it, often without the nuance and context required. This constant search to acquire more also comes from a place of feeling not good enough or less than, or feeling entitled, much of which can be traced back to traumatic and colonialist experiences and roots.

3. **Racism:** Acquisition can be intermingled with race, where white people seek to (again, subconsciously or consciously) dominate and degrade people of color. In the feminist arena, this tendency can be further complicated if a person who is of color has been abused by a white person - or vice versa - and they now carry a deep bias against all people who are similar to their abuser. This kind of bias can be dangerous in the workplace, often creating situations where the biased person is triggered by an innocuous comment or event. Their unhealed wounds can cause havoc for well-meaning feminists without any warning. Racism creates many challenges, and solves none.

4. **Subtle discrediting:** In settings where one would expect feminists to support each other, there can often be the opposite: overt encouragement but subtle discrediting that is mixed in with the praise. There can also be a desire to point out flaws or mistakes as a way to

feel superior to the other feminist. Yet again, feminists can come across as needing to put their sisters down in order to feel good about themselves. As girls, we are brought up to take care of others and be selfless and self-deprecating. Sadly, this can often result in mean behaviors among grown women, including feminists, who are not exempt from this deeply ingrained childhood conditioning and are acting out of pent up resentment and frustration about their ability to understand their own worth.

5. **Defiant rebellion:** While making a show of supporting each other verbally, feminists can vehemently oppose each other through their behavior. For example, they may verbally congratulate a feminist on her achievements, while disrespecting her through the way they treat her in professional settings - undermining, deprioritizing, and finding other ways to put her, her work, and value down. Unless a person is grounded in who they are, this kind of behavior, as well as the discrediting, can be very

damaging to one's mental and emotional health, and the ongoing stress can eventually manifest in physical ailments.

6. **Judgment:** Feminists can be quick to pass judgments on each other - whether it's judging their appearances, work, or skills. They might be quick to say they would have done things differently, to throw doubt into a person's mind about the task or approach. These judgments can accumulate and hurt the person being attacked, unless they are strong in their sense of self and their professional practices.

7. **Gossip:** Feminists can be notorious gossips, talking behind each other's backs both immediately after an occurrence or years later. While feminists may tout the importance of being vulnerable, they may adopt a patriarchal stance to look down on the feminist who showed vulnerability and talk about them in a degrading manner. Needless to say, this can be very hurtful to the one who showed vulnerability

8. **Emotional Stunting:** Feminists may champion self-care and vulnerability, but they may be the first to be stoic vessels of bottled emotion, never showing any sadness, grief or tears. They may not relate well with people who show emotion because they equate emotions to weakness - a classic patriarchal trait - or they've had such a traumatic event in the past that they have shut down emotionally.

Sometimes, as we can see with these examples, feminists, just like anyone else, can be trapped in traumatic childhood patterns that cause them to be assholes in the workplace.

However, because they are feminists, their assholery is amplified in contrast to their chosen values of feminism: equality, empathy, inclusion, collective care, and respect. It is no wonder that women who are harmed by feminists might want to leave the movement. And, toxic feminists can create a negative reputation for all feminists as angry and hateful, which is absolutely not the case.

Ultimately, I always come back to my mantra: we cannot bring about in the world that which we cannot nurture in ourselves. In other words: we cannot defeat patriarchy, capitalism and colonialism if we carry them deep in our traumatized hearts and psyches.

We must uproot these tendencies within first, and then have a viable hope of creating a freer, kinder, more equal, and more loving world.

Reflection:

Which of these reasons for feminists being assholes have you experienced? What did it feel like?

Notes:

45

Part III   Bridgerton Case Studies with Pacific Spotlights

"Why must our only options be to squawk and settle or to never leave the nest? What if I want to fly?"

Eloise Bridgerton

48

Before beginning this section, I highly recommend watching Bridgerton seasons 1 and 2 on Netflix, if you have not done so already. The show provides many opportunities for shifts in thinking about how the world could be. I also reflect in these case studies about Pacific examples of feminists I have encountered, without identifying them, of course.

Case Study 1: Tracing Trauma Patterns

I watched Bridgerton seasons 1 and 2 for the second time, which is rare for me. Aside from being a massive Jane Austen fan, I've been intrigued by how well trauma patterns[12] and feminist themes are portrayed in the Bridgerton franchise, and the high quality acting. I've not read Julia Quinn's books, so my analyses are limited to the Netflix show.

Bridgerton depicts a world similar to Jane Austen's – the Regency era - with a focus on how difficult it is for women to maintain a virtuous reputation so they may attain a good husband who can provide for them financially. In this time, elites did not work, but had fortunes bequeathed to them, or estates where others worked the land for them. Women were not allowed to own property or inherit, hence their dependence upon marriage. This life was the focus of Austen's famous novel, *Pride and Prejudice*. While Bridgerton follows a similar theme, the departure happens with people of color in high society, including the Queen herself. In the world of Bridgerton, which I think

---

[12] Check out my trauma book, entitled *From Abused to Empowered: Recognizing and Releasing Behavior Patterns that come from Trauma*:
https://amzn.to/3ryQCa6

is a world resolutely heading for feminism, we see characters grappling with patriarchy in their own ways and overcoming them beautifully.

Both seasons of Bridgerton depict the male protagonists struggling with trauma, which love helps heal: this will be the focus of the first case study. In the second one, I'll examine the feminist characters and how they challenge the toxic patriarchy. Then I will take a look in the third case study at what happens when women have too much masculine energy – as many feminists do.

Here's my perspective on how trauma shapes the two leading men in seasons 1 and 2 (spoiler alerts):

Father Wound

In the first season, the Duke of Hastings, Simon Basset, is plagued by his harsh father's inability to accept him. Simon loses his mother at birth and grows up with a stammer, which fuels his already-grieving father's rage. At his father's deathbed, Simon swears that he will never sire an heir, so the family's lineage can end with him.

Thus, Simon's relationships with women consist of sex only. When he meets, falls for, and marries Daphne Bridgerton, Simon sticks to his vow, and feels conflicted and guilty, because Daphne's dream is to have a family. It's clear that he loves children, but he stubbornly sticks to his vow for some time.

Simon shows some of the characteristics of a father wound – rigid boundaries, anger, and low confidence.[13] Eventually, through his new wife Daphne's unconditional love, Simon learns that he need not be perfect, and that he need not continue lashing out at his dead father. They conceive, and presumably live happily ever after – indeed, Simon does not appear in season 2, but Daphne and baby Augie do and all seems quite well.

Post-Traumatic Stress Disorder

When we get to season 2, the Viscount Anthony Bridgerton, who has spent most of his adulthood fulfilling family duties – because his father died suddenly when Anthony was a teenager – begins looking for a wife. Prior to this, he had a love affair with a soprano singer, and then followed the same pattern as Simon of no-strings sex with multiple women. The two men are great friends – no surprise there.

---

[13] For more on the father wound, see: https://tinyurl.com/2s43bznt

When Anthony meets Kate Sharma, he engages in activities with her, like riding and hunting, that remind him of his father. Significantly, when Kate is stung by a bee, Anthony experiences a panic attack, because his father died from a bee sting. Experiencing this trigger in Kate's presence helps him bond with her as she soothes him.

Anthony has a lot of trouble expressing his emotions due to the trauma of his father's death.[14] His mother's devastation thereafter has left him too afraid to pursue true love. It takes a near-death experience – Kate's accident – for Anthony to admit his love, and to finally express his feelings to Kate. It is interesting too that Kate shares some of Anthony's characteristic emotional suppression, because she too lost her father and has served as the support system for her family.

In both cases, the male protagonists' journey involves healing their trauma and opening their hearts to love. Daphne is seen as the quintessential young woman in season 1, but with the persistence it takes to make her marriage work, despite her mother, Lady

---

[14] Learn more about the effects of early parental death: https://tinyurl.com/59yy3jcs

Bridgerton's feeble attempts to prepare her for marriage, sex, and pregnancy.

In season 2, a similar character appears in the form of Edwina Sharma – Kate's younger sister – but Kate shines brighter and is as accomplished as Anthony in many ways (hunting, riding and so on), symbolizing a shift from season 1 and a deeper look at feminist empowerment toward equality – read more about this in the next case study.

Reflection:

Simon, Anthony and Kate portrayed emotional wounds that impacted their relationships. What emotional wounds do you think you are carrying? How might you heal?

Notes:

PACIFIC SPOTLIGHT

In the Pacific, relationships are ubiquitously impacted by trauma. Domestic violence is rampant, and provides a stark example of severe trauma. Indeed, where I currently live, in Fiji, the numbers are alarming. The pattern I've seen as a trauma coach is that men, who are socially conditioned to bottle up emotions and never speak about abuse, turn to alcohol, drugs and other ills as coping mechanisms, and abuse their significant others physically and sexually when their pent up trauma explodes as rage. There is also emotional, verbal and psychological abuse to keep the women subjugated.

Women too are conditioned to never speak about abuse, but they also are brainwashed into being doormats and caregivers, so they do not focus on or prioritize their own needs. Hence, they become repositories of abuse, low confidence, little self-esteem, and diminished opportunities, despite being talented and resilient. While some women have broken out of this, many women remain trapped in these situation. It doesn't help that some feminist leaders in Fiji with significant power are also abusive.

The combined disasters posed by COVID 19 and tropical cyclones in Fiji led to a rise in domestic violence, which was not surprising given Fiji's history, but at the same time posed an alarming third crisis. However, women-owned businesses also proliferated, indicating the resilience and creativity women possess. Incubators and other supportive organizations helped these women bring their goods to market, and the economy still boasts some of these amazing products, including vegan and gluten-free treats, jewelry, handicrafts, and more.

In a country like Fiji where counseling services are limited and still stigmatized, many women are able to succeed when they need to step up and take charge – how much better could they do if they receive the support they need? Marginalized people in the LGBTQIA+ communities such as sex workers are receiving support from women's funds, and slowly becoming more empowered.

There are local toxic "feminists" within the women's movement and neocolonial feminists in the development sector who assume they know better – the good news is there is also a rising majority of younger feminists who embody true feminist principles and are seeking to do good despite the patriarchal onslaught from the toxic, patriarchal and colonialist "feminist" forces.

Despite the difficulties posed by entrenched patriarchy and toxic "feminists" who sabotage Fiji's feminist movement, some wins are now becoming visible. In the Pacific, we have our work cut out for us, and breaking the silence to tell our stories will be a necessary and powerful first step for people of any gender. It is time to break away from harmful patriarchal patterns so each person, of any gender, can flourish.

Reflection:

Do you think trauma patterns are universal, or different based on culture? Why?

What do you think has been the role of colonialists and missionaries in influencing how Pacific people deal with trauma?

Notes:

Case Study 2: 7 Lessons from Feisty Feminists

In the previous case study, I took a look at the trauma patterns of the two leading men in the franchise so far: Simon Basset and Anthony Bridgerton. In this one, I examine the seven feminist characters that I enjoyed across both seasons.

These women really raised the bar for the Regency era in unique ways that left the men stumped sometimes. Of course, there are other female characters who stay in the system and try to work with it, like Lady Bridgerton, Lady Featherington, Lady Cowper and Cressida Cowper. However, the characters who work to break the patriarchal systems that confine them are much more interesting. Let's get to these seven feisty feminists and the lessons they bring (spoiler alerts):

1. **Fighting against tradition: Daphne Bridgerton.** Although we see Daphne's character as initially succumbing to society's pressures to come out into society and find a husband, which she does as the season's diamond, Daphne is wise and complex. She wants to explore life. She seeks to understand and face situations, such as trying out

self-pleasure, wanting to know how babies are conceived, chastising her mother for not giving her education about sex, challenging her husband lovingly to overcome his trauma, and working hard to make her marriage work. She tires of men, including her brother Anthony, who think they know what's best for her. In wanting to chart her own course amid social pressure, Daphne earns the title of budding feminist. She teaches us that *it's okay to challenge traditional parenting, especially when it harms you or your loved ones.*

2. **Graceful and Subtle Wisdom: Edwina Sharma.** Although, like Daphne, Edwina appears at first to be docile and conforming to society's demands she follows Daphne's path and becomes the diamond of season 2. Edwina seeks to secure Anthony as a husband because of the secure life he can give her, but she carries a quiet independence too. She is well-educated and loves her own company. She speaks to Anthony of being content in her own pursuits, which evidences a wise and detached approach to romance that few young women could muster under those social conditions and at that age. In her balance

between being agreeable and self-assured, Edwina subtly shines as someone with the potential to be a rule-breaker. When she soothes the King, she reveals wisdom beyond her years. When she gives a pep talk each to Kate and Anthony in church, she reveals how her authenticity has overcome her desire to fit in. She shows us that *it's important to be in a loving relationship with yourself so you don't depend on anyone else for your happiness.*

3. **Feminist Intellectual and Rebel: Eloise Bridgerton.** Eloise cannot be examined without attention to her extreme social anxiety. Yet her most endearing qualities are her sharp tongue and confident exposure of all the patriarchal woes plaguing women: women are treated as inferior; they are expected to display themselves and attract a rich husband, marry and bear children; women cannot own property or make decisions. Eloise is the equivalent of the feminist activist at a rally who wields the megaphone: she is blunt and unafraid to raise important feminist issues. Eloise helps us see that *it's important to be informed, critical and to challenge the status quo for*

women as the first step of forging a better way.

4. **Stealth Gossip Stirrer: Penelope Featherington, also known as Lady Whistledown.** Penelope appears, on the surface, the weakest of the weak in terms of societal status. She is the daughter of a cunning woman, youngest of three sisters, overweight, and mostly the wallflower who is overlooked at balls and other gatherings. The exception is her friend Eloise, with whom Penelope shares a deep friendship. Penelope is in love with Colin Bridgerton, who is in love with Marina Thompson. So, Penelope bears the pain of unrequited love. However, Penelope is admirable and powerful as Lady Whistledown, writing her column filled with her observations in society. Information is her power, as the content she publishes carries the power to influence everyone who reads it. She is also a great example of a prolific female entrepreneur, who, at a tender age, is accumulating money from the sale of her publications. Penelope, through her role as Lady Whistledown, demonstrates that *power can be held in any position if we have the right information and know how to use it.*

5. **Woman of Mystery: Genevieve DelaCroix.** No one really knows the history behind this modiste (dressmaker) with the fake French accent, but Madam DelaCroix makes her mark as an entrepreneur, a sexually liberated woman, and a most valuable ally to Lady Whistledown. She is a creative person who quietly controls her life, saying no when she wants, and wielding power in an understated way. She hints that in a world where we are able to refrain from our typical prejudices, *sexual liberation and strong boundaries are desirable traits in a feminist woman leader.*

6. **Feminist Strategist: Lady Danbury.** On the surface, Lady Danbury is a widow with a limp, which may sound unremarkable and even pitiful. However, she is the woman who raised Simon, helped him overcome his stammer and maintain ethical leadership as a duke; influenced the Queen on multiple occasions (including having her name Edwina Sharma as the season's diamond in Season 2); helped Kate come to terms with her feelings; and displayed considerable matchmaking prowess. She is a woman of power, who is confident,

wealthy (owning her own estate as Bridgerton breaks the rules of patriarchal Regency norms), and very aware of the privilege granted to people of color by the now mentally ill king. She's a wonderful example of feminist leadership that is strong, strategic, and wise. She teaches us that *strategy and influence are crucial markers of good leadership.*

7. **Brown and Bold Badass: Kate (Kathani) Sharma.** Kate comes along and blasts men's notions of women to smithereens in season 2 of Bridgerton. She grew up in India where she learned to ride, shoot and hunt, and can basically match wits with anyone. She is confident, discerning, outspoken, and undeterred by patriarchal constraints (although she is over-masculinized, and I will address this in the next case study). She is not afraid to call Anthony out, for instance, when he scoffs at her shooting ability before they go hunting. The act of a brown woman challenging a white man of some nobility, is wonderful to behold. She is also stoically single, carrying the burden of society's judgments. To be sure, she does eventually marry, but Kate does life on her own terms (Anthony concedes that he must humble himself

before her) and that is badass indeed. Kate role models what it's like to *be a feminist: treat everyone as an equal, and demand to be treated as an equal too.*

These feminist characters and the archetypes they begin to portray, make Bridgerton irresistible to me, because of the change being brought to this historically patriarchal world – the Regency era. The lessons learned, are powerful and we can apply them to the present day.

Reflection:

Think of the feminists you know – do any of them fall into these archetypes and if so, how?

Which lesson resonates the most with you from the list in this case study? What does this tell you about yourself?

Notes:

PACIFIC SPOTLIGHT

In the Pacific, there are feminists I've had the pleasure of working with who embody some of the characteristics of these characters. The Feminist Strategist is an archetype I have seen in my country. I've been working with her for a few years now – she is a master at feminist strategy, fundraising, and relationship building who also brings the most empathic of hearts – a beautiful combination in a leader and a great asset to the Pacific region.

Another example I've had the honor to know well is the embodiment of the Brown and Bold Badass – she is a leader at a very high level who is outspoken and pioneering – always uplifting other women as she journeys to greater heights. Her thinking is razor sharp and she creates pathways that allow other aspiring leaders to bring to fruition a feminist future.

These women are rare gems in the Pacific, where the feminist movement tends to be marred with toxic "feminists" who carry with them their past abuse, and actively torture other women in the movement. It will take time to bring healing to these abusive women – and only if they agree there is a problem with their approach. People with abusive tendencies who deliberately manipulate others rarely seek help, so the outlook might be bleak. Indeed, these toxic "feminists" have been wielding power over younger generations of feminists for a long time. Hope does reside, however, in the hearts and minds of younger generations who are stepping up to take carry the torch of true feminism.

Reflection:

What do you think it would take for a toxic "feminist" to ask for help to heal?

Notes:

Case Study 3: Excessive Masculine Energy

In the two previous case studies, I analyzed trauma patterns in the male protagonists, and looked at the somewhat archetypal and certainly feisty feminist characters and the lessons they offered, respectively. In this post, I focus on Kate Sharma, the female protagonist in season 2. Yes, spoiler alert here too.

Kate's character depicts a woman who is initially overbalanced in her masculine energy. She shoots and hunts, rides and behaves just like a man of nobility: discerning, confident, and quick to voice her opinion in a decisive manner.

The loss of her parents and her desire to protect and provide for her half-sister Edwina and Edwina's mother, Lady Mary, propel Kate into overdrive when it comes to masculine energy. Indeed, she behaves just like Anthony Bridgerton in some ways.

In season 1, Anthony watches his sister Daphne's suitors like a hawk, turning almost all of them away. In season 2, Kate displays a similar tendency to protect her sister Edwina, wanting to steer her away from Anthony and anyone else who seems less than genuine. The main similarity is that both Anthony and Kate are acting out of a sense of duty, due to each of them losing their father. This leads them to act in rigid, controlling ways, a sign of the toxic masculine.

Kate also displays anger, frustration, and a tendency to block her emotions, due to the post-traumatic stress of losing her parents. Again, this is similar to Anthony's journey as a character. Their similar life experience is also probably why they are so attracted to each other – they are both living in ways that are disconnected from their own hearts. They are both also grieving and afraid to love and be hurt deeply again.

As they fall in love, Kate fights her emotions. However, with time, after her accident, and after many reassurances from Edwina, Lady Mary, and Lady Danbury, Kate is able to open her heart and tap into her feminine qualities. She finds her flow as a feminine person by accepting Anthony's love. This begins when she agrees to dance with him, and they share a few playful and romantic moments on the dance floor.

Kate's journey from masculine to feminine is chronicled symbolically through the color of her costumes: she is wearing dark shades of blue, teal, and purple while hunting, riding, and chaperoning Edwina. Later in the series, as she fights her growing feelings, she wears lilac, lavender, orange, silver, and cream; these warmer and lighter colors signal the softening of her heart.

When a woman has an overbalance of masculine energy, it is difficult for her to open up to a man romantically. She tends to repel masculine men, and attract feminine men who need saving.

A truly masculine man can take charge, be supportive, respect boundaries, and provide consistent love. This is the type of man Anthony realizes he must become in order to honor Kate. In his second proposal, Anthony expresses his love and intention to humble himself, which provides the safety and reliability Kate needs to release her masculine coping tendencies, open up her heart, and accept him.

These experiences can be true for people of any gender because we all have inner masculine and feminine energies that need to be in balance. This balance helps us attract a partner who is similarly well-adjusted.

Reflection:

How balanced are you in terms of your inner masculine and feminine energies?

What would more balance allow you to do that you are currently afraid to do or otherwise not doing?

Notes:

PACIFIC SPOTLIGHT

Inevitably, I've found that people attract each other like jigsaw-shaped magnets based on their trauma. This is because we can only attract the same resonant frequency that we emit. If we are traumatized, we will attract the same. Once we are healing at a deep level, we will attract those who are also doing deep healing work.

In the Pacific, I've noticed many feminists who have too much masculine energy. This could be because of their past abuse, being single mothers who must provide for their children, and a host of other reasons. While being overbalanced in masculine energy can help women achieve their goals as providers, because it makes them stoic and focused on the practical instead of the emotional, it can also block them from balancing themselves and being open to feminine qualities such as receptivity, flow, and creativity.

As a result, such overbalanced women attract feminine partners who look to them for leadership. This basically means their relationships are arenas where each partner's trauma plays out over and over. It isn't an authentic or balanced relationship; it is founded upon trauma patterns.

Another example is the type of couple that is together because each of their self-fulfilling prophecies is based on the need for safety. They are hiding from what they fear most in the world. Often, these types of relationships can be between a heterosexual woman who is afraid of aggression, and a homosexual man who is afraid to be outed. They come together, both closeted and scared to openly talk about the overwhelming need to stay safe and hidden that is driving their relationship choices.

In many villages and cities across the Pacific, the widely accepted and somewhat capitalistic norm is to get married, settle down and have children, buy a home and other material luxuries and do better than your neighbor. People tend to follow this so closely that they don't realize why they are doing it – it just is a huge driving force in their reality. Much later, these automatons wake up, get divorced and begin to find themselves. The awakening happens because we are masked by trauma, and relationships must change or fall away when we recognize the masks, decide to remove them and understand the person underneath.

Of course, in the Pacific, there is social pressure to stay together, so the divorce option is a road less taken, resulting in many affairs, half-siblings, and messy family configurations that can remain hidden for years. Men often feel entitled to having a family on the side because it is a social norm. The pain of revealing these illicit relationships can break families and marriages apart, unless Pacific people practice the old norm of not speaking about it. The cycle is vicious, and contains a lot of pain.

Reflection:

How could the Pacific Region benefit from more awareness around trauma and the imbalance of inner masculine and feminine energies?

How might feminists incorporate more trauma-informed approaches in their work to help women, men, and non-binary people heal?

Notes:

Gaps and A Way Forward

Gaps in Feminist Work in the Pacific

This year, I attended the Pacific Update at the Laucala Campus, University of the South Pacific (USP) in Suva, Fiji. It was eye-opening, with dynamic speakers and interesting topics. I attended two gender panels on Day 1, and learned a lot about intimate partner violence (IPV) in Samoa, gender financing in the Pacific, digital financial products available to women in the Pacific via the United Nations Capacity Development Fund (UNCDF), the Pacific Girl program, Toksave[15] (a most excellent gender research portal), and how Pacific Women Lead operates.

I learned that "gender transformative practices' is another way of saying "feminist work", which is interesting. There was talk of the divide between academics and practitioners, and the need to build stronger bridges so language and ideas can be more easily shared, and collaboration can be smoother. As it turned out, in each panel, I asked a question that came to mind while listening to the panelist's presentations. Both my questions revealed gaps

---

[15] Check it out: https://www.toksavepacificgender.net/

in research that are interesting to me. Let me explain.

LGBTQIA+ focus and funding is missing in gender work in the Pacific region.

When the first panel ended, I asked for the mic and asked this question: "Is there research being done to track financing, IPV, and provision of financial products during times of disaster to people in the LGBTQIA+ communities in the Pacific? Could you describe any work you are doing or know of?"

The answer from all panelists was that they are not focused on this. They are looking at gender and people with disabilities, or families (in the case of IPV in Samoa). From the responses of panelists, it didn't sound like they were going to add this area to their work. It is a glaring gap, and this makes me wonder why. Why aren't we focusing on this very vulnerable and marginalized community?

There are amazing non-governmental organizations in Fiji that work with these communities, including Women's Fund Fiji and DIVA. So, why isn't this community being included in the Pacific regional discussions on gender financing, disaster insurance, and other gender-sensitive areas of study and implementation – it's not like people from the LGBTQIA+ communities aren't affected by disasters, so why aren't they being supported?

Trauma is not explicitly or comprehensively addressed in a lot of gender work.

The second panel was really interesting. I asked something like: "Adolescent girls encounter trauma in their families, for example when they witness or experience abuse, and when they are bullied at school. Is there a trauma component in all the work you've been discussing?" I wanted to know if there was a focus on trauma as part of the 170 million-dollar investment on gender that is being implemented through the Secretariat of the Pacific Community (SPC) and other non-profit organizations.

The answers were that while trauma isn't talked about, it is the fundamental reason the women's movement exists. While there are some initiatives on cyber bullying within the Pacific Girl program, there isn't any major focus on trauma. Neither is there a specific trauma focus in the Toksave research portal.

I am curious about why trauma is not explicitly addressed – it is indeed a root level topic that requires a lot of capacity to handle well. It would be interesting to see what a focus on trauma would look like, in the context of gender, patriarchy and colonialism – historical and current. There are some initiatives in Fiji that work on trauma or hint at it, for example counseling services through non-profits and the Ministry of Health, or the archives that list the *girmitiyas*[16] who were brought to Fiji and encountered atrocities they never expected.

Inclusion of LGBTQIA+ communities, in my mind, is an essential step to gain a more complete picture of what is happening through a gender lens, and likewise, addressing trauma at a root level is critical to healing patriarchal and colonial wounds of men, women and non-binary people, as well as in addressing domestic, gender-based, and intimate partner violence. I hope to see more attention to these two gaps in the future for the Pacific, which is known for its high rates of homophobia and violence against women and girls.

As a practitioner who integrates across several fields, including gender, climate change, leadership, and design, I am always thinking about inclusion and root causes. To me, many of the current wicked problems like climate

---

[16] Indentured laborers brought to Fiji by the British from India.

change, racism, gender inequality, and poverty cannot be solved without addressing the underlying trauma patterns and working on the intersectionality of the issues.

Reflection:

What are your priorities for conducting or supporting feminist work where you live?

What are the barriers, and what would support you?

Notes:

The Soul of Feminism

We are local beings living in an increasingly global world. We can reach each other instantly using the Internet and yet we are lonelier than ever before. It is crucial that we understand who we are and what kind of world we want to create.

We are all different in some way from one another, so the quest to create a world in which differences are embraced and celebrated can be a universal and uniting factor. Why not have a world where you can be valued and treated equally, regardless of your gender, skin color, race, ethnicity and social class? Why not be a real feminist, and eliminate all forms of inequality?

Of course, it's not that easy. The underlying trauma work takes time and is excruciatingly difficult. We must commit to uprooting patterns that don't serve humanity or the planet, and transition to ways of thinking and behaving that nurture life instead of creating divisiveness. This is a significant part of the feminist struggle and to be sure it is an intersectional one.

To create a better world, we must embody a better self, and the essence of what it means to be a real feminist. What is the soul of feminism?

It is to bring forth and anchor the qualities that can bring transformative change to the world. These include being empathic, just, principled, ever-learning, boundary-conscious, visionary, self-loving, trauma-informed, healing, sharing power, and being relentless as we pursue a world of peace, justice, and compassion. Let's look at what these terms mean in this context:

Empathic: we must extend genuine empathy to all we encounter. This means understanding, validating and caring about the other party's point of view and experience. It does not mean taking on the other person's emotions, burdens and perspectives or trying to please them at the expense of yourself.

Just: To be just includes being aware of what might be virtuous versus vicious pathways and choosing what would help create more fairness in the situation than what is currently present, to the extent we can envision that. It means to do the things that promote equity and equality.

Principled: It is crucial to be aware of our own values and to live according to the principles that emerge from those values. For instance, if we value empathy then we practice caring for each other genuinely.

Ever-Learning: We refrain from judgment, but seek to understand other points of view. We experiment and try new things except those actions that violate our principles. We don't assume we know, but stay flexible and adaptive so we can keep learning.

Boundary-Conscious: We remain acutely aware of what is acceptable and unacceptable to us, what is safe and what is a violation. We set strong boundaries and honor them. We also adapt our boundaries as we evolve and as conditions change.

Visionary: We keep our passion for justice and peace alive and work from that, infusing all our work with that fire as we work toward a world that is peaceful and just.

Self-Loving: We do the inner work it takes to become our own best friends, and practice self-love and self-care as a foundational priority. This does not mean becoming arrogant or narcissistic, but rather becoming attuned to how best to nourish and care for ourselves so that we can thrive more of the time.

Trauma-Informed: We educate ourselves on trauma patterns and are aware of how they operate underneath our work situations. We practice empathy and understanding when encountering trauma and set strong boundaries to eliminate abuse.

Healing: We maintain our inner work, to heal from our own trauma, triggers, biases and judgments, so that we can become more open-minded and peace-loving.

Sharing Power: Once we are on our healing journey, we can shift from wanting power and control, which comes from the ego, to sharing power with others instead of wielding power over others. This includes working collaboratively to co-create and be co-responsible for new structures and systems that nurture feminist ways of living and working.

Relentless: We nurture ourselves to maintain a resilient mindset and stay on the path to transformative change, ushering in an era of true feminism, peace and justice. Resilience in mind, body, heart and spirit are necessary to face and remove the deeply ingrained patriarchy we all still live in.

It begins with me, and I am still working on myself. My inner work, learning, work with feminists, and the guidance I provide to clients has made this book possible as a reflexive snapshot in time.

I hope my journey so far has brought you to a different place than where you began. Let's continue learning – in an ever-changing world, it's our best strategy.

With all my love,
Marilyn

Reflection:

What does the soul of feminism mean to you and what motivates you to embody that?

What would you add to the list of qualities and why?

Notes:

ABOUT THE AUTHOR

Marilyn Cornelius is a behavior change specialist, coach, facilitator, author, teacher, and speaker. She supports leaders to help address climate change and wellness challenges through her multinational company, Alchemus Prime. Marilyn integrates behavioral sciences, design thinking, biomimicry and meditation techniques in novel ways using Alchemus Prime's Diamond Model. Marilyn's work implements her vision for how to live and lead in ways that are authentic, resource-efficient, adaptive to change, empowered and beneficial to all living beings.

Marilyn has authored or co-authored 36 other popular books on self-love, trauma, and positivity. She holds a PhD in behavioral sciences and climate change from Stanford University. She has taken courses in Heartfulness, Vipassana, Mindfulness-Based Stress Reduction (MBSR), and Transcendental Meditation (TM). Marilyn has been a Reiki Master since 2009. She has served as Chief of Staff and Coach at UN Women USA. Marilyn's free services on social media include "Mornings with Marilyn," a daily video show on positivity and empowerment; a weekly series called "Beyond Medicine"; and Dr. An, a cantankerous trauma doctor who gives an-swers.